Languages of the World

Hindi

Anita Ganeri

Heinemann Library
Chicago, Illinois

www.heinemannraintree.com
Visit our website to find out more information about Heinemann-Raintree books.

To order:
☏ Phone 888-454-2279
▭ Visit www.heinemannraintree.com to browse our catalog and order online.

Edited by Dan Nunn, Rebecca Rissman, and
   Catherine Veitch
Designed by Marcus Bell
Picture research by Ruth Blair
Production by Victoria Fitzgerald
Originated by Capstone Global Library Ltd
Printed and bound in China by South China Printing
   Company Ltd

15 14 13 12 11
10 9 8 7 6 5 4 3 2 1

Library of Congress Cataloging-in-Publication Data

Ganeri, Anita, 1961-
   Hindi / Anita Ganeri.
      p. cm.—(Languages of the world)
   Includes bibliographical references and index.
   ISBN 978-1-4329-5081-1—ISBN 978-1-4329-5088-0 (pbk.) 1. Hindi language—Textbooks for foreign speakers—English. 2. Hindi language—Grammar. 3. Hindi language—Spoken Hindi. I. Title.
   PK1933.G26 2012
   491.4'382421—dc22   2010043785

Acknowledgments

We would like to thank the following for permission to reproduce photographs: Alamy pp. 5, 19 (© Neil McAllister), 9 (© The Print Collector), 11 (© Image Source), 12 (© Stephen Ford), 21 (© Dinodia Photos), 22 (Design Pics Inc.), 23 (© Friedrich Stark), 24 (© Chris Fredriksson), 25 (© Tim Gainey), 26 (© Simon Reddy), 28 (© Dean Mitchell), 29 (PhotosIndia.com LLC); Corbis p. 15 (© Kevin Dodge); Shutterstock pp. 6 (© Jakub Cejpek), 7 (© Paul Prescott), 8 (Tarasenko Sergey), 10 (Kharidehal Abhirama Ashwin), 13 (© absolute-india), 14 (© michaeljung), 16 (jaimaa), 17 (absolute-india), 18 (© Sam Dcruz), 20, 27 (© Aleksandar Todorovic).

Cover photograph of a boy reproduced with permission of Photolibrary (India Picture).

We would like to thank Shkeela Cooper for her invaluable help in the preparation of this book.

Every effort has been made to contact copyright holders of material reproduced in this book. Any omissions will be rectified in subsequent printings if notice is given to the publisher.

All the Internet addresses (URLs) given in this book were valid at the time of going to press. However, due to the dynamic nature of the Internet, some addresses may have changed, or sites may have changed or ceased to exist since publication. While the author and publisher regret any inconvenience this may cause readers, no responsibility for any such changes can be accepted by either the author or the publisher.

Contents

Hindi words are in italics, *like this*. You can find out how to say them by looking in the pronunciation guide.

Hindi Around the World

Hindi is mainly spoken in India, especially in the north and center of the country. It is the main language of India.

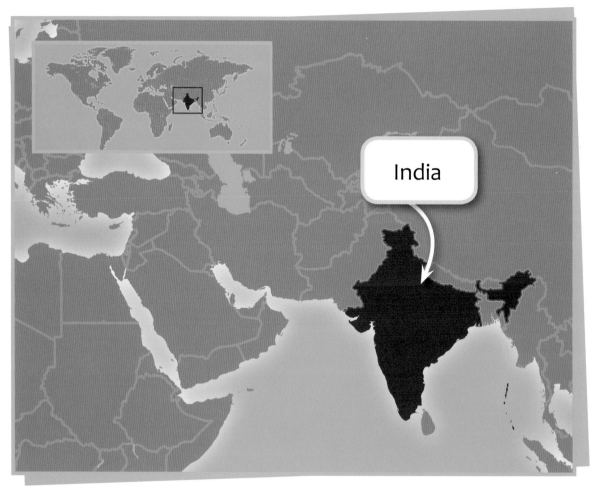

India

How to say it
India = *bhārat*
Hindi = *hindī*
language = *bhāṣā*

People also speak Hindi in Fiji, Mauritius, and in countries where Indians have gone to live. These are places such as Britain, Canada, and the United States.

Who Speaks Hindi?

More than 500 million people around the world speak Hindi. It is one of the most spoken languages in the world.

India is a crowded country with millions of people.

Many Indians speak several languages.

India has 22 main languages. Hindi is one of the most important. Many Indians speak Hindi and several other Indian languages as well.

Hindi and English

Hindi comes from an old language called Sanskrit. No one speaks Sanskrit any more, but some Sanskrit words are still used in Hindi.

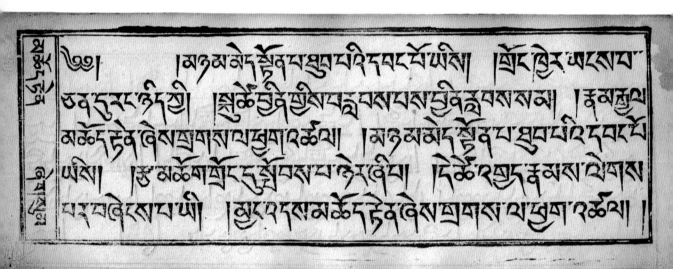

Sanskrit is read from right to left, unlike English, which is read from left to right.

King George V and Queen Mary visit Delhi, India.

The British ruled India in the 19th century and the first half of the 20th century. During this time some Hindi words began to be used in English. These include *bangle*, *bungalow*, *cheetah*, *cot*, *jungle*, *pajamas*, and *shampoo*.

Learning Hindi

Hindi is written in a different alphabet from English. The letters in a word are linked by a line across the top. Some of the sounds in Hindi are very different from English.

न हान क कारण फोड़, दाद, त्वचा प
ता है । यह स्थिति बहुत तकलीफदेह
हीं होती है । इसके लिए नीम का
इए । नीम के पत्तों को लगभग 200
। तांबे के बर्तन में 500 मि. ली
उठने लगे तब यह चटनी उसमें डाल
में पीला मोम जरा सा एवं जरा सा
यह मलहम की शक्ल में आ जाये
तियों को पानी मे उबाल कर इस

The best way to learn Hindi is to listen to people speaking Hindi and try to copy them.

In this book, Hindi words are written in the same alphabet that is used to write English. This makes them easier for you to read. The extra marks on some of the letters show how the words should sound.

Saying Hello and Goodbye

When Hindi speakers meet they put their hands together and say "*Namaste.*" This shows respect. It is also how people say "Goodbye."

How to say it
hello = *namaste*
goodbye = *namaste*

How to say it

How are you? = *Tum kaise ho?* (to a boy)
How are you? = *Tum kaisī ho?* (to a girl)
I'm fine = *Maiṁ ṭhīk hūṅ*
okay, fine = *ṭhīk hai*

To ask someone how they are you say
"*Tum kaise ho?*" to a boy, or "*Tum kaisī
ho?*" to a girl. To reply you might say
"*Maiṁ ṭhīk hūṅ*" or "*ṭhīk hai,*" meaning
"okay" or "fine."

Talking About Yourself

To tell someone your name you might say "*Merā nām … hai*" ("My name is … "). To tell them how old you are you might say "*Maiṁ das sāl kā hūṅ*" ("I am ten years old").

How to say it
My name is … = *Merā nām … hai*
I am … years old = *Maiṁ … sāl kā hūṅ*

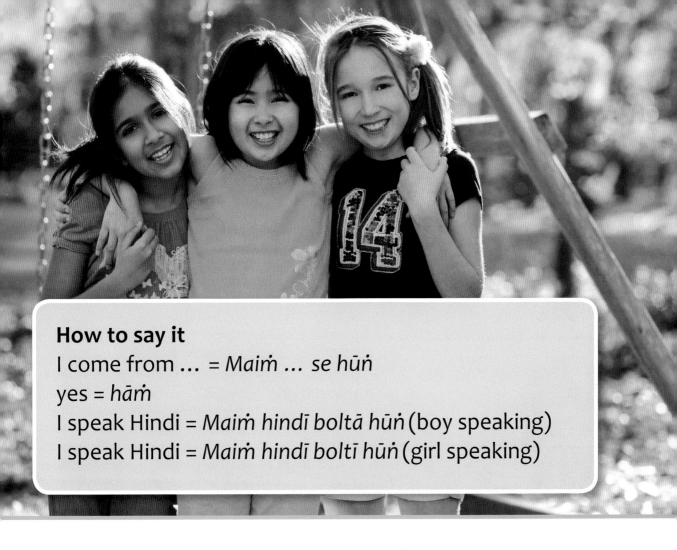

How to say it

I come from … = *Maiṁ … se hūṅ*

yes = *hāṁ*

I speak Hindi = *Maiṁ hindī boltā hūṅ* (boy speaking)

I speak Hindi = *Maiṁ hindī boltī hūṅ* (girl speaking)

If someone tells you they are from India they might say "*Maiṁ bhārat se hūṅ.*" If they ask you if you speak Hindi you can say, "*Hāṁ, maim hindī boltā hūṅ*" if you are a boy, or "*Hāṁ, maim hindī boltī hūṅ*" if you are a girl.

Asking About Others

There are different ways of saying "you" in Hindi. Calling someone *āp* is polite and shows respect. You can use *tum* for people your own age or friends. This book uses *tum*. *Tumhārā* means "your."

How to say it
What is your name? = *Tumhārā nām kyā hai?*
How old are you? = *Tumhārī umar kyā hai?*

How to say it

Where do you come from? = *Tum kahāṅ se ho?*
Do you speak Hindi? = *Kyā tum hindī bolte/boltī ho?*

If you want to ask where someone is from you ask "*Tum kahāṅ se ho?*" To ask if they speak Hindi you say "*Kyā tum hindī bolte ho?*" if it's a boy, or "*Kyā tum hindī boltī ho?*" if it's a girl.

At Home

In India, people's homes can be very different. Indian cities are busy, crowded places. In cities, many people live in large apartment buildings.

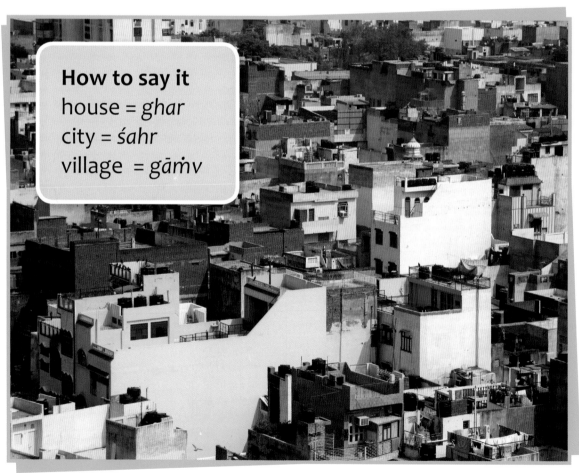

How to say it
house = *ghar*
city = *śahr*
village = *gāṁv*

How to say it
room = *kamrā*
window = *khiṛkhī*
door = *darvāzā*

In the countryside, people often live in villages. They work by farming the land. Village homes are usually small and simple.

19

Family Life

In India, people often have large families. People use different words for different members of their families. It depends on whether they are younger, older, or on their mother's or father's sides.

How to say it
family = *parivār*
parents = *mātā-pitā*

How to say it
mother = *mātā*
father = *pitā*
brother = *bhāī*
sister = *bahn*
grandfather = *dādā*
    (father's father)
grandmother = *dādī*
    (father's mother)

In many Indian families, grandparents, parents, aunts, uncles, and children all live together in the same home. They help to look after each other. They keep each other company.

At School

In India, children start school when they are six years old. But some children from poor families have to leave school early to go to work.

How to say it
book = *kitāb*
pen = *qalam*

Some schools have modern buildings and classrooms. But village schools may be held in the open air, with children sitting on the ground.

Having Fun

People in India like doing many different things in their spare time. Every day, millions of people go to movie theaters to see the latest movies. People also like listening to Indian music.

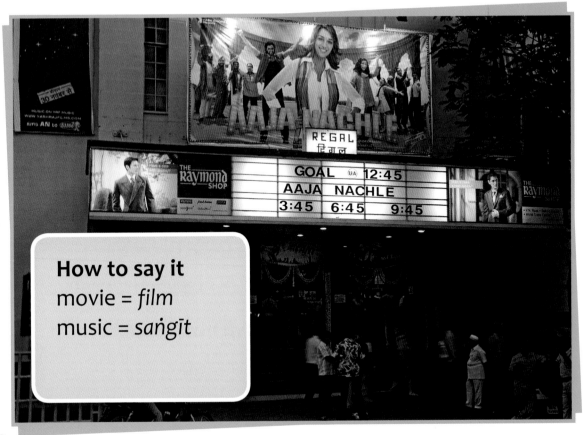

How to say it
movie = *film*
music = *saṅgīt*

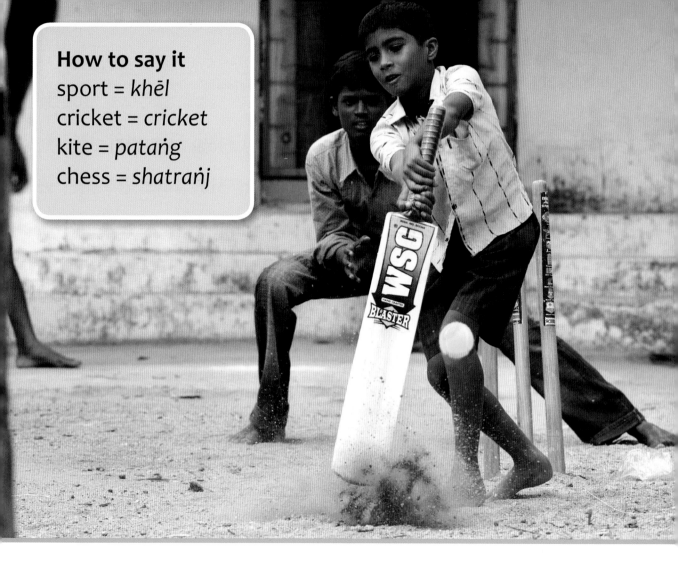

Sports are very important. Many Indians, like the boys in the photo, love cricket. They also like flying kites and playing chess. Teams also take part in an Indian game, called *kabaddi*.

Food and Drink

Indian food is famous around the world. There are many Indian restaurants in most countries where Indians have gone to live. Most Hindi speakers are vegetarians and do not eat meat.

How to say it
bread = *rotī*
rice = *chāval*
vegetables = *sabzī*

How to say it
yogurt = *dahī*
sweet = *miṭhāī*
water = *pānī*

People like to eat spicy vegetables, a
thick, lentil soup called *dhal*, yogurt,
and rice or flat breads, such as *chapattis*.
Indian sweets are very popular. There is
usually water to drink.

Clothes

What clothes do you like wearing? Many people in India wear the same sort of clothes as you do, for example jeans and T-shirts. In Hindi, the word for "clothes" is *kapṛe*.

How to say it
clothes = *kapṛe*
jeans = *jīns*
T-shirt = *tī shirt*

How to say it
sari = *sāṛī*
shirt = *kurtā*
trousers (cotton) = *pājāmā*

Many Indian people also wear traditional Indian clothes. A woman wears a *sāṛī* that is made from a long piece of material. A man wears cotton trousers and a long shirt, called a *kurtā*.

Pronunciation Guide

English	Hindi	Pronunciation
book	*kitāb*	*kitaab*
boy	*laṛkā*	*larkaa*
bread/chapatti	*roṭī*	*rowtee*
brother	*bhāī*	*bhaee*
chess	*shatraṅj*	*shutranj*
city	*śahr*	*shuhur*
class	*klās*	*klaas*
clothes	*kapṛe*	*kupray*
cricket	*cricket*	*crickit*
door	*darvāzā*	*durvaazaa*
Do you speak Hindi?	*Kyā tum hindī bolte ho?* (boy)	*Kyaa tum hindee boltay ho?*
	Kyā tum hindī boltī ho? (girl)	*Kyaa tum hindee boltee ho?*
family	*parivār*	*purivaar*
father	*pitā*	*pitaa*
fine, okay	*ṭhīk hai*	*teek hay*
girl	*larkī*	*lurkee*
goodbye	*namaste*	*namastay*
grandfather	*dādā*	*daadaa*
grandmother	*dādī*	*daadee*
hello	*namaste*	*namastay*
Hindi	*hindī*	*hindee*
house	*ghar*	*ghur*
How are you?	*Tum kaise ho?* (boy)	*Tum kaysay ho?*
How are you?	*Tum kaisī ho?* (girl)	*Tum kaysee ho?*
How old are you?	*Tumhārī umar kyā hai?*	*Tumharii umur kyaa hay?*
I'm fine	*Maiṁ ṭhīk hūṅ*	*Mai teek hoo*
I am … years old	*Maiṁ … sāl kā hūṅ*	*Mai …saal kaa hoo*
I come from …	*Maiṁ … se hūṅ*	*Mai …say hoo*
I speak …	*Maiṁ … boltā hūṅ* (boy)	*Mai …boltaa hoo*

I speak ...	*Maiṁ ... boltī hūṅ (girl)*	*Mai ... boltee hoo*
India	*bhārat*	*bhaarat*
jeans	*jīns*	*jeens*
kite	*pataṅg*	*putung*
language	*bhāṣā*	*bhaashaa*
man	*ādmī*	*aadmee*
mother	*mātā*	*maataa*
movie	*film*	*film*
music	*saṅgīt*	*sungeet*
My name is ...	*Merā nām ... hai*	*Meraa naam... hay*
parents	*mātā-pitā*	*maataa-pitaa*
pen	*qalam*	*kulum*
rice	*chāval*	*chaawul*
room	*kamrā*	*kumraa*
sari	*sāṛī*	*saaree*
school	*skūl*	*skool*
shirt	*kurtā*	*koortaa*
sister	*bahn*	*behn*
sport	*khēl*	*khayl*
sweet	*mithāī*	*mitaaee*
teacher	*adhyāpak*	*adheeyaapuk*
ten	*das*	*duss*
trousers (cotton)	*pājāmā*	*paajaamaa*
T-shirt	*tī shirt*	*tee shirt*
vegetables	*sabzī*	*subzee*
village	*gāṁv*	*gaaw*
water	*pānī*	*paanee*
What is your name?	*Tumhārā nām kyā hai?*	*Tumhaaraa naam kyaa hay?*
Where do you come from?	*Tum kahāṅ se ho?*	*Tum kuhaan say ho?*
window	*khiṛkhī*	*khirkhee*
woman	*aurat*	*orut*
yes	*hāṁ*	*haam*

Find Out More

Books

Parker, Vic. *We're from India*. Chicago: Heinemann Library, 2006.
Roop, Peter and Connie. *A Visit to India*. Chicago: Heinemann Library, 2008.

Website

kids.nationalgeographic.com/kids/places/find/india

Index